¡Nuestra maravillosa Tierra!
Our Exciting Earth!

DESIERTOS
DESERTS

Claire Romaine
traducido por / translated by Eida de la Vega

Please visit our website, www.garethstevens.com. For a free color catalog of all our high-quality books, call toll free 1-800-542-2595 or fax 1-877-542-2596.

Cataloging-in-Publication Data

Names: Romaine, Claire.
Title: Deserts = Desiertos / Claire Romaine.
Description: New York : Gareth Stevens Publishing, 2018. | Series: Our exciting Earth! = ¡Nuestra maravillosa Tierra! | In English and Spanish. | Includes index.
Identifiers: ISBN 9781538215371 (library bound)
Subjects: LCSH: Deserts–Juvenile literature. | Desert ecology–Juvenile literature.
Classification: LCC GB611.R65 2018 | DDC 577.54–dc23

Published in 2018 by
Gareth Stevens Publishing
111 East 14th Street, Suite 349
New York, NY 10003

Translator: Eida de la Vega
Editorial Director, Spanish: Nathalie Beullens-Maoui
Editor, English: Therese Shea
Designer: Bethany Perl

Photo credits: Cover, p. 1, 17 Anton Foltin/Shutterstock.com; p. 5 Ilyshev Dmitry/Shutterstock.com; p. 7 totajla/Shutterstock.com; p. 9 Diego Delso/Wikipedia.org; p. 11 NadyaEugene/Shutterstock.com; p. 13 KajzrPhotography/Shutterstock.com; p. 15 B Norris/Shutterstock.com; p. 19 EcoPrint/Shutterstock.com; p. 21 Jenn_C/Shutterstock.com; p. 23 hadynyah/E+/Getty Images.

Printed in the United States of America

CPSIA compliance information: Batch #CW18GS: For further information contact Gareth Stevens, New York, New York at 1-800-542-2595.

Contenido

Vamos a visitar el desierto 4
El más grande 12
Plantas del desierto 14
Animales del desierto 18
Palabras que debes aprender 24
Índice 24

Contents

Visit the Desert! 4
The Biggest 12
Desert Plants 14
Desert Animals. 18
Words to Know 24
Index. 24

¡Vamos al desierto!

....

Let's go to a desert!

Los desiertos no
tienen mucha agua.
Cae poca lluvia.

•••••••••••••••••••••••••••••••

Deserts don't
have much water.
They get little rain.

Algunos desiertos
tienen arena.
Otros tienen rocas.

....

Some deserts
have sand.
Some have rocks.

Algunos desiertos
son calientes.
¡Otros son fríos!

....

Some deserts are hot.
Some are cold!

El desierto caliente
más grande está
en África.

....

The biggest hot
desert is in Africa.

Algunas plantas
viven en el desierto.
Pueden vivir
con poca agua.

....

Some plants live
in deserts.
They can live
without much water.

Los cactus tienen piel dura que los ayuda a guardar agua.

....

Cactus have tough skin to keep in water.

Algunos animales
viven en los desiertos.
Algunos se esconden
del sol.

Some animals live
in deserts.
Some hide
from the sun.

¡Veo burros!
Comen plantas para
obtener agua.

....

I see donkeys!
They eat plants
for water.

Monto un camello.
¡Los desiertos son divertidos!

....

I ride a camel.
Deserts are fun!

Palabras que debes aprender
Words to Know

(el) cactus
cactus

(el) camello
camel

(el) burro
donkey

Índice / Index

África / Africa 12

animales / animals 18

lluvia / rain 6

plantas / plants 14, 20